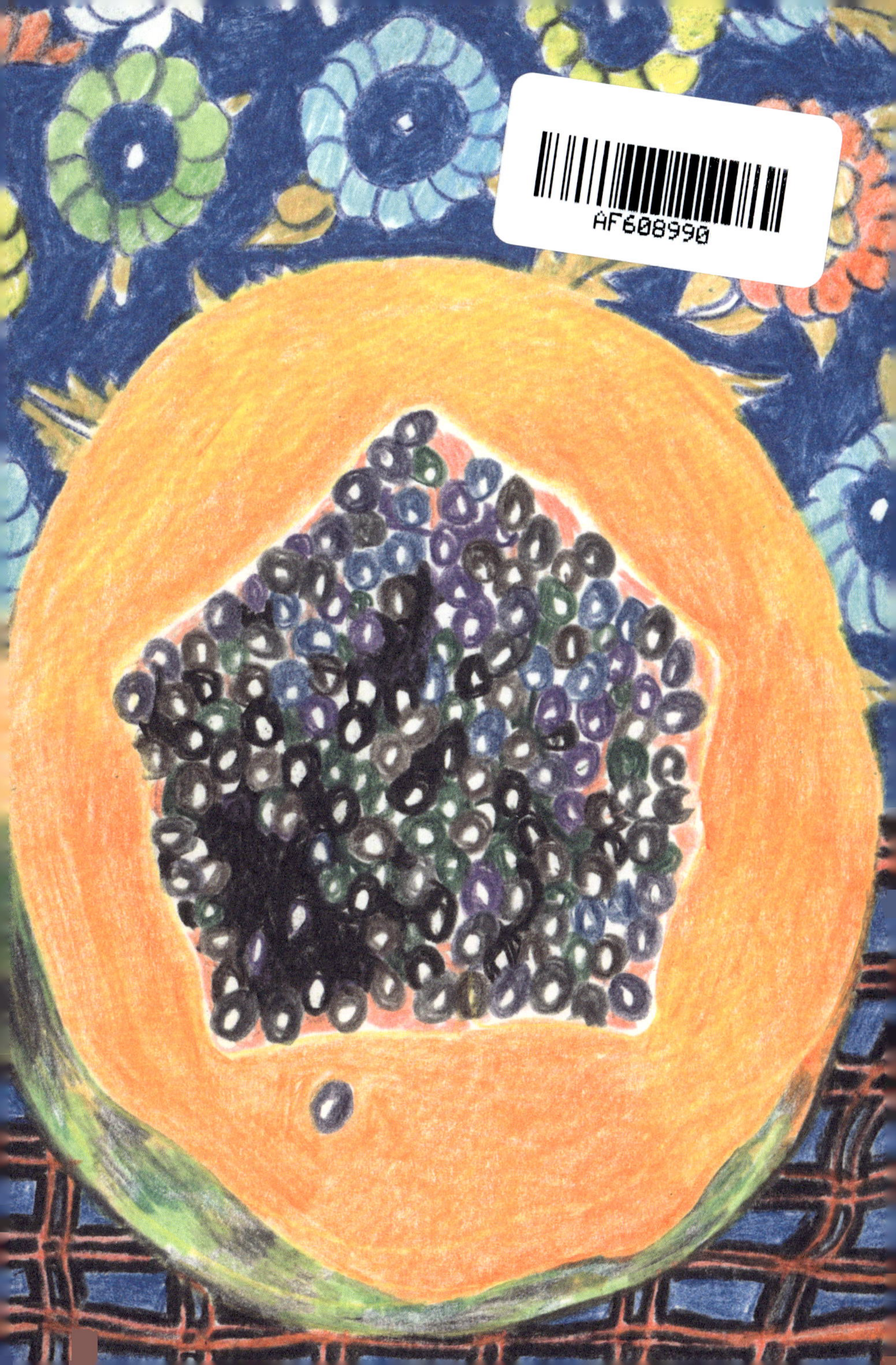

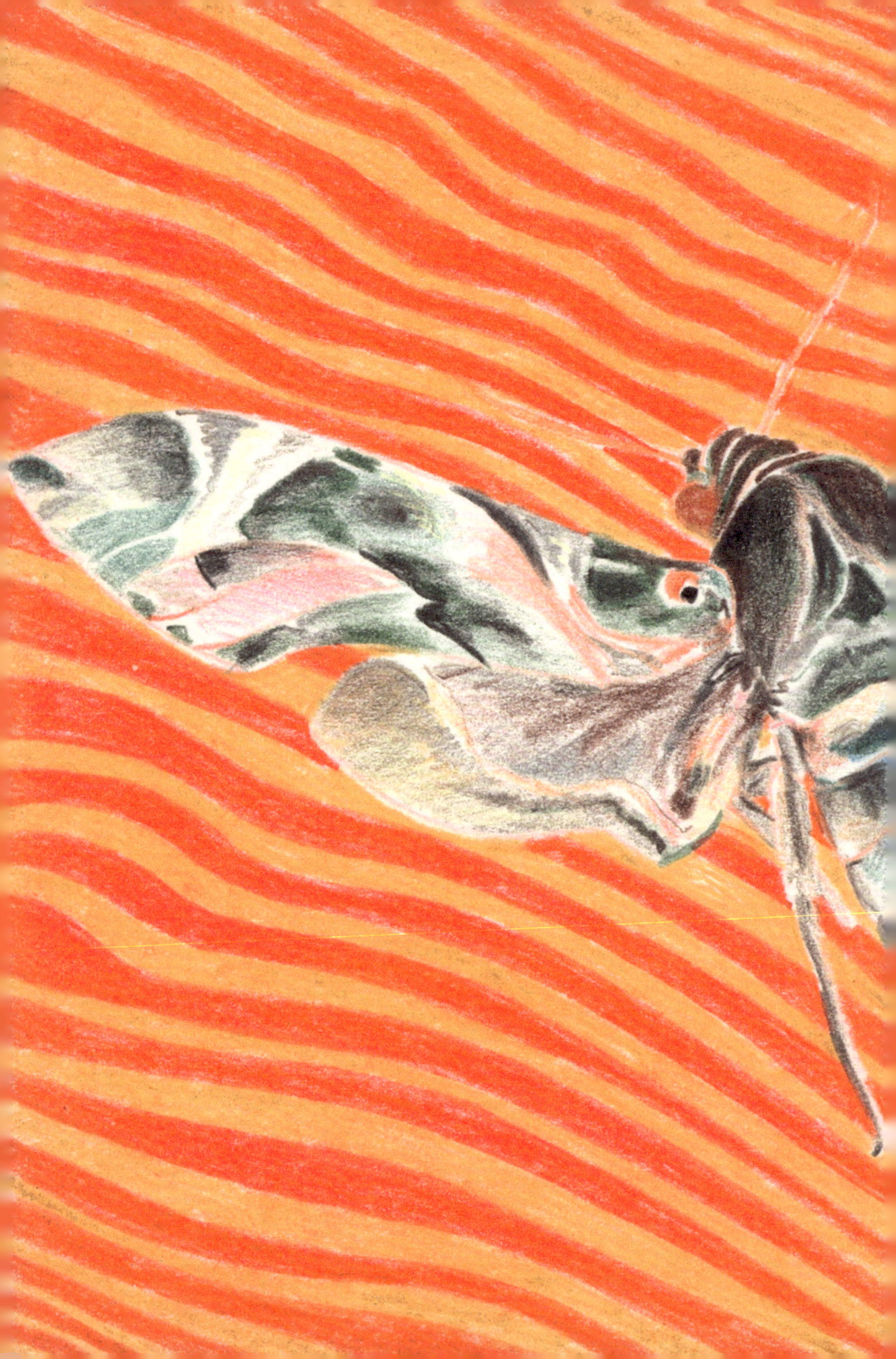

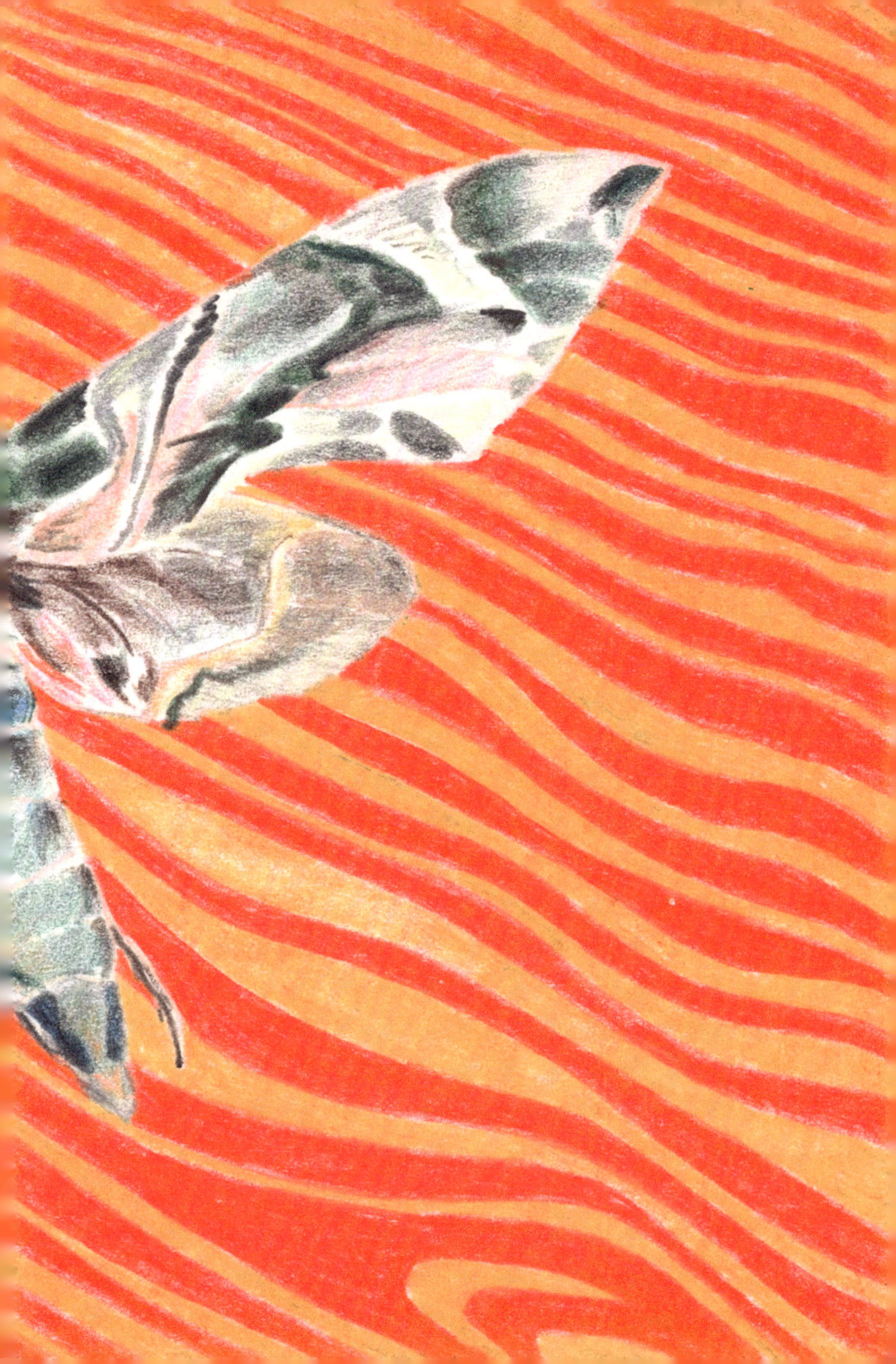

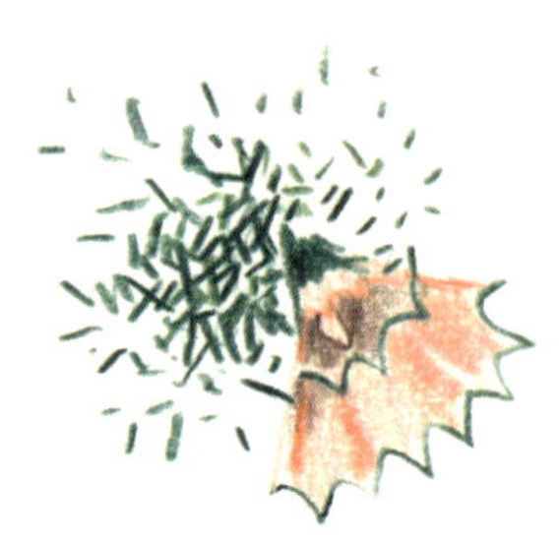

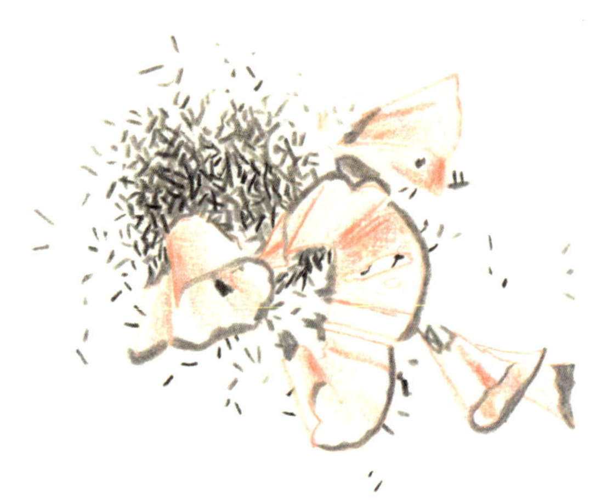

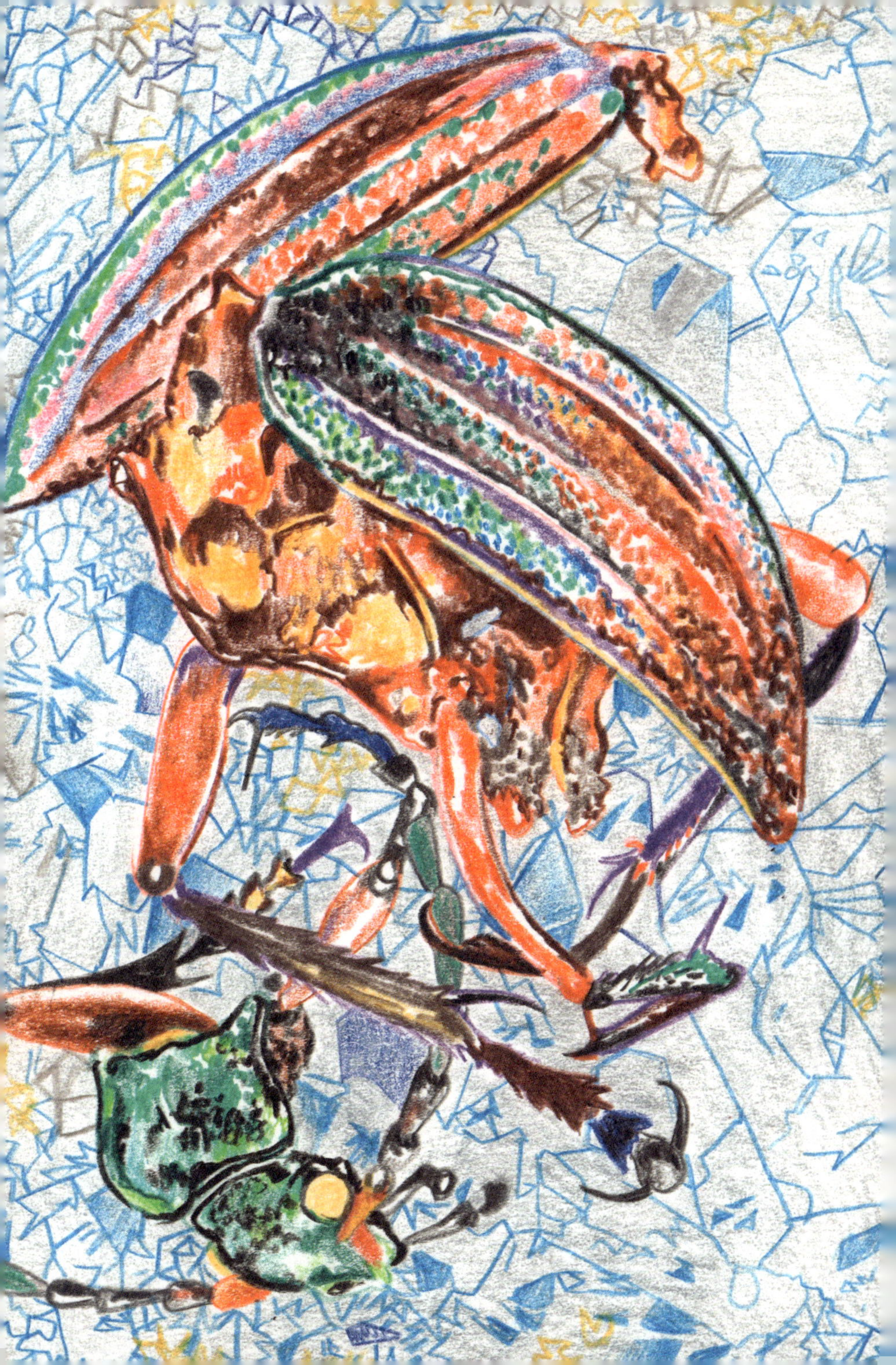

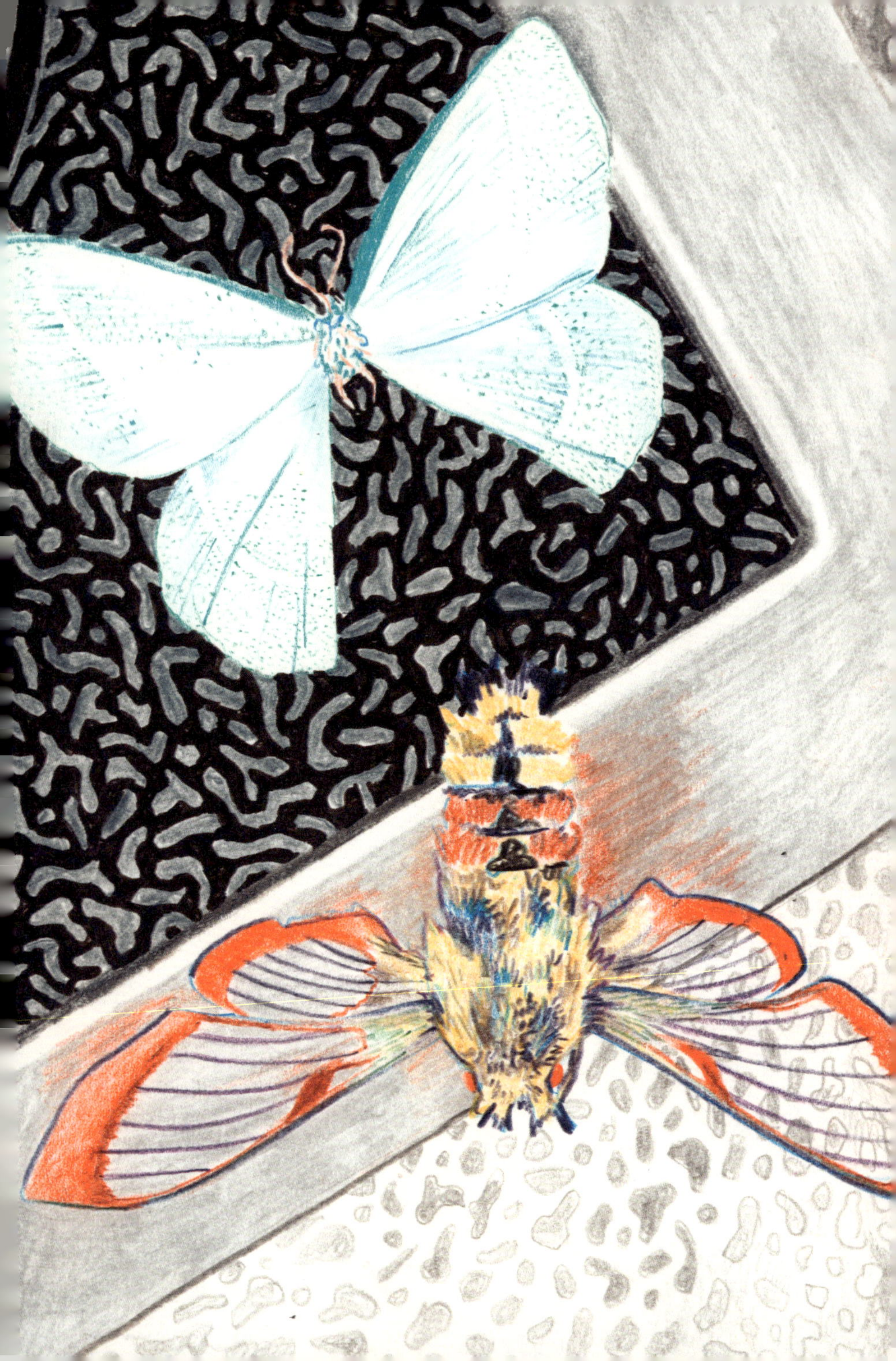

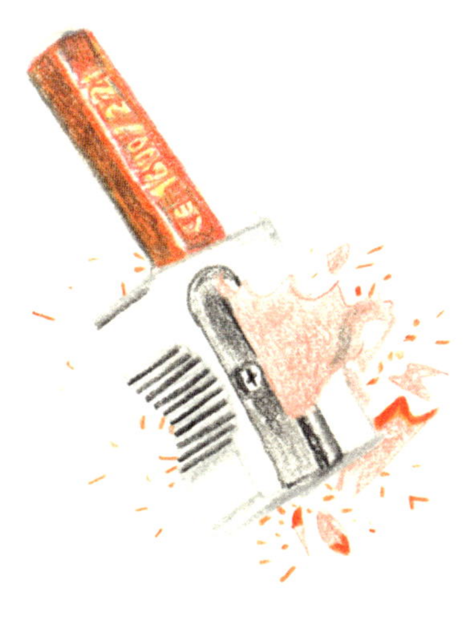

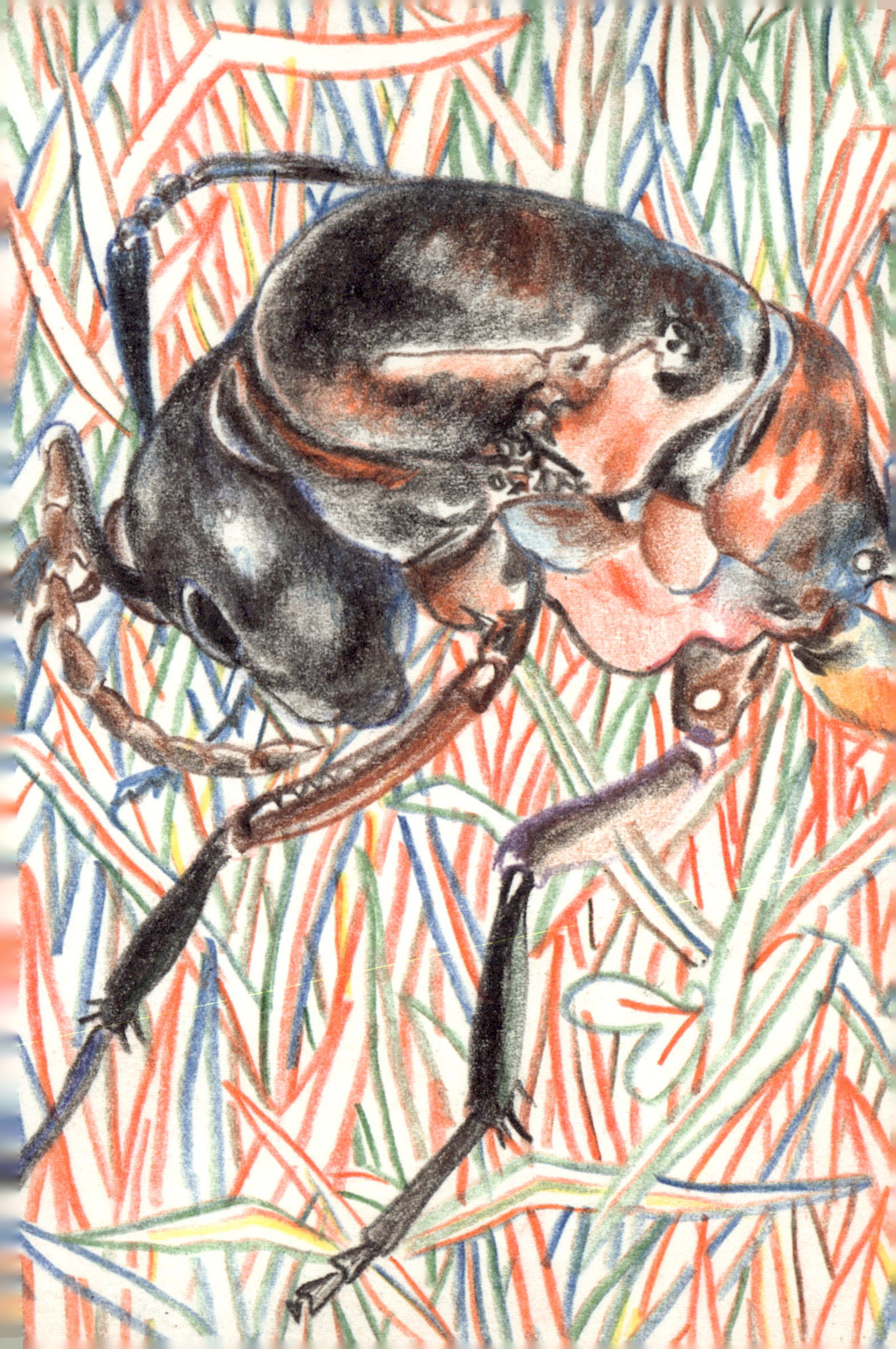

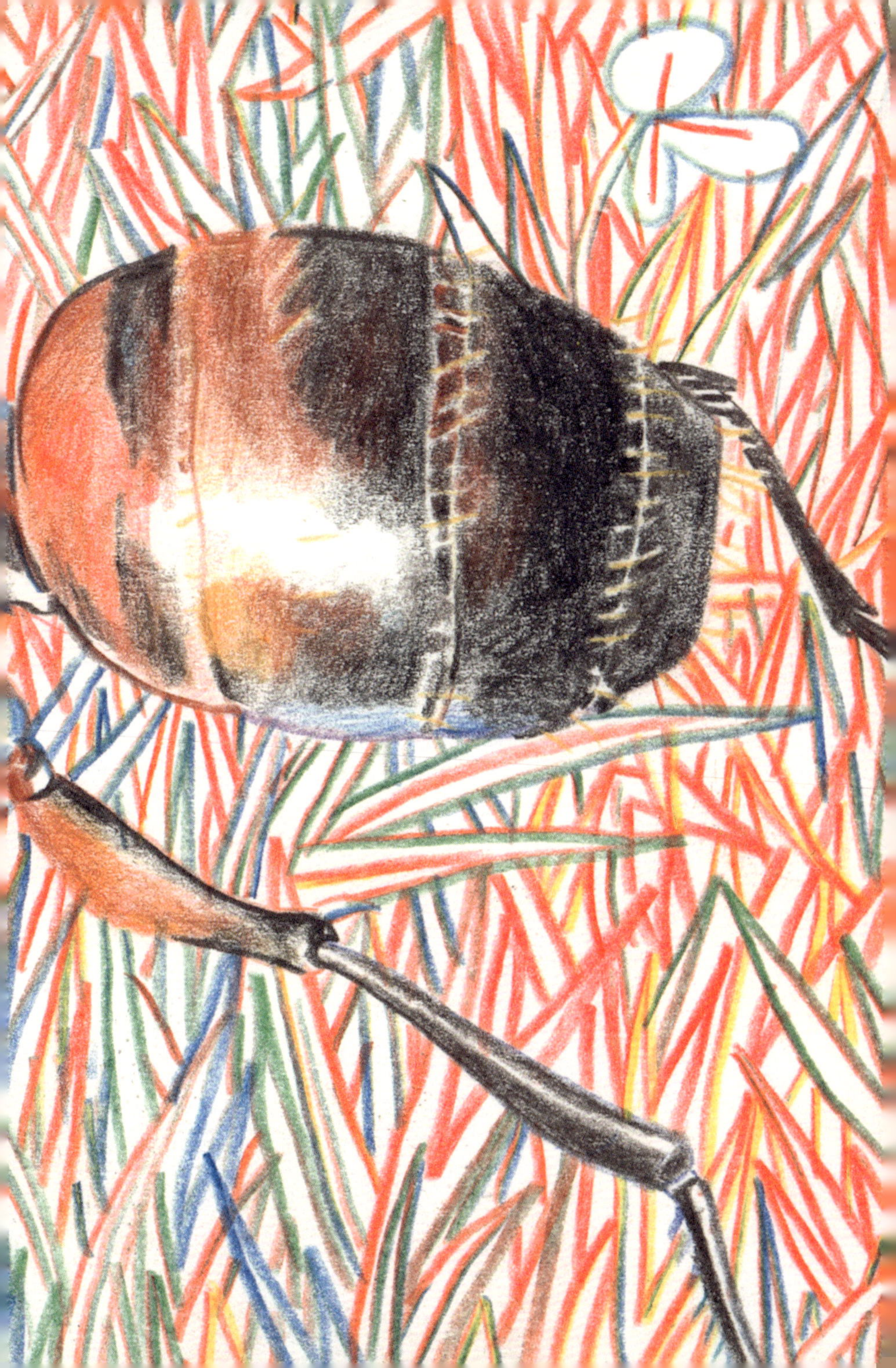

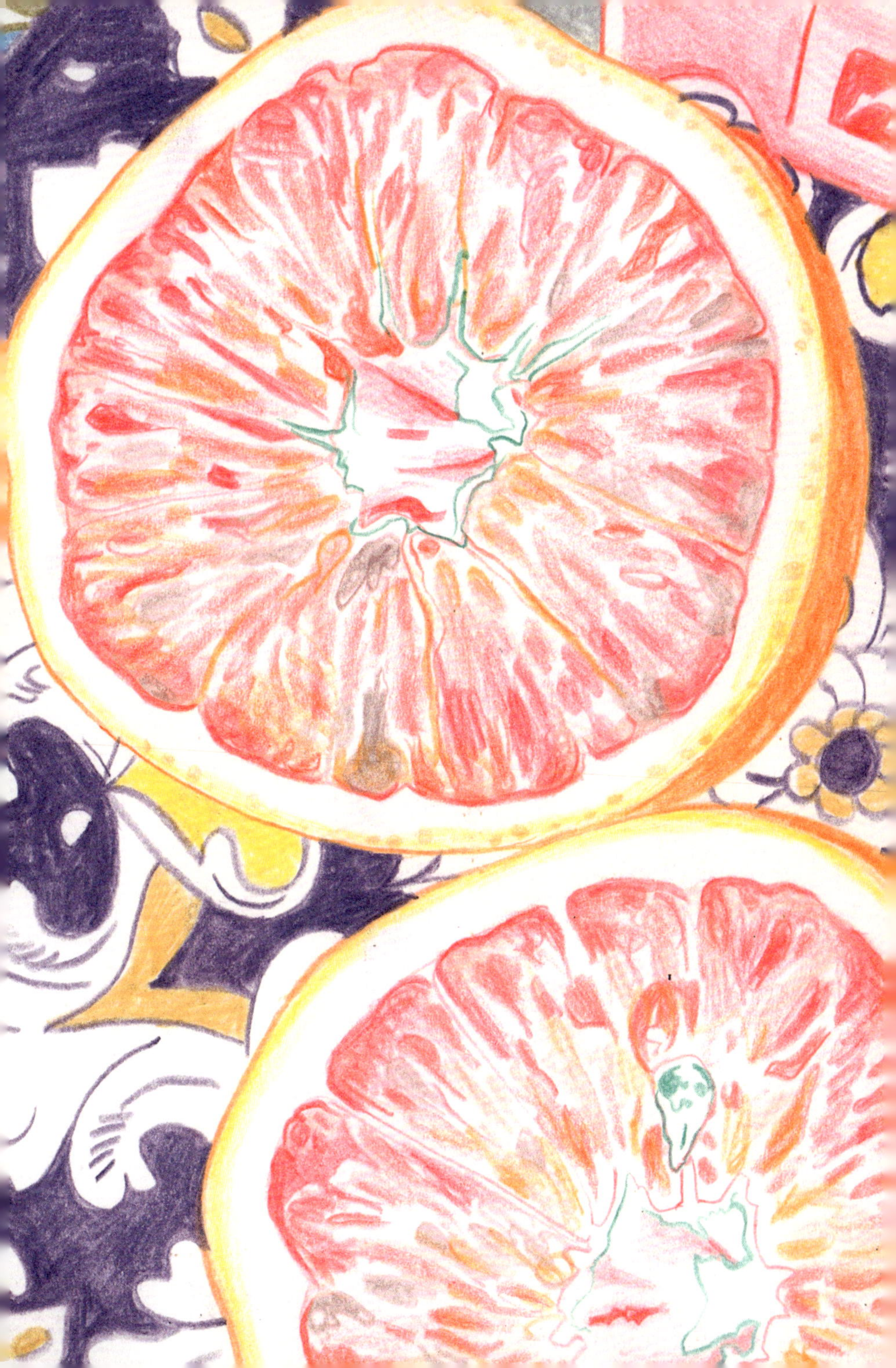

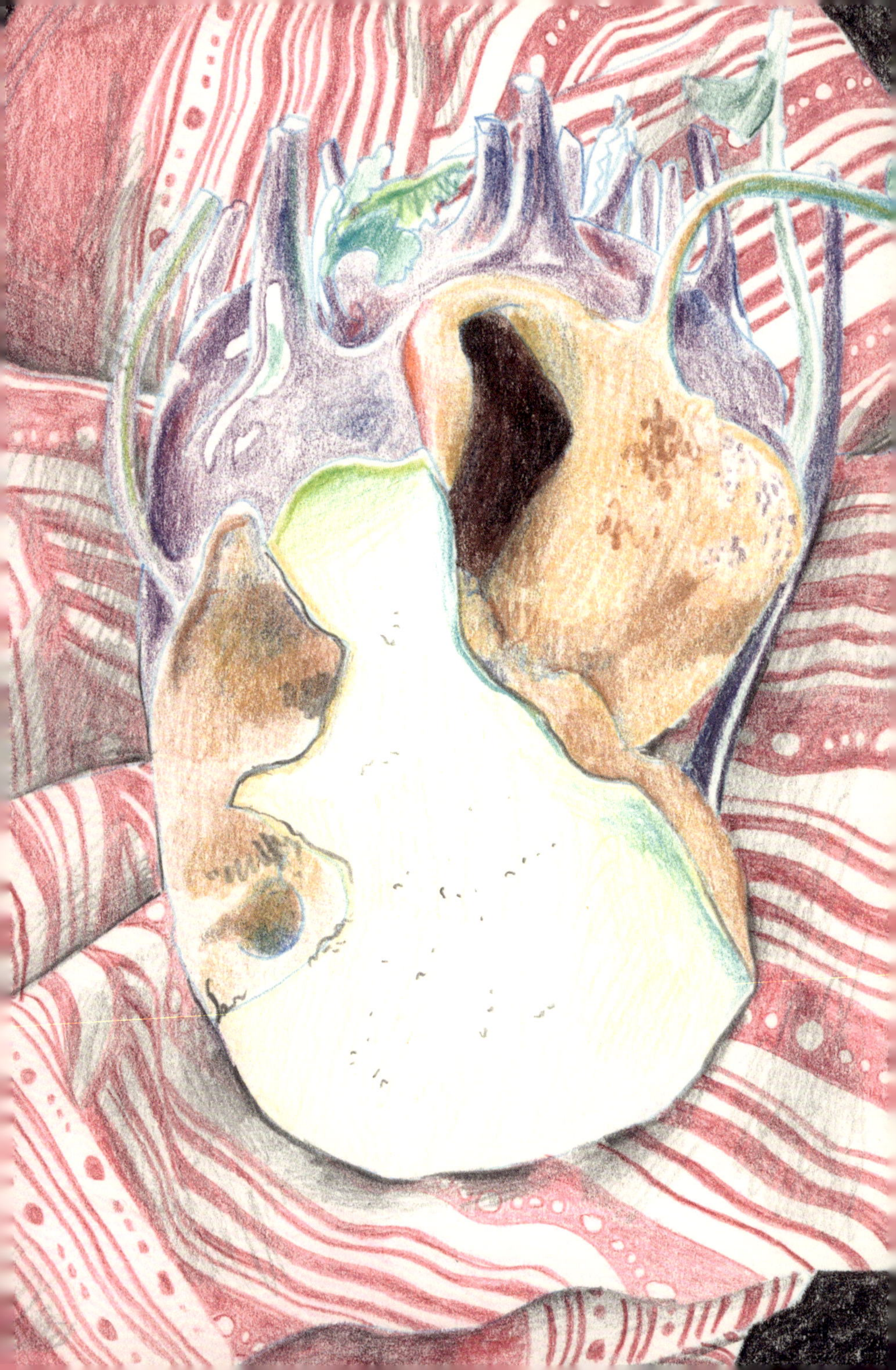

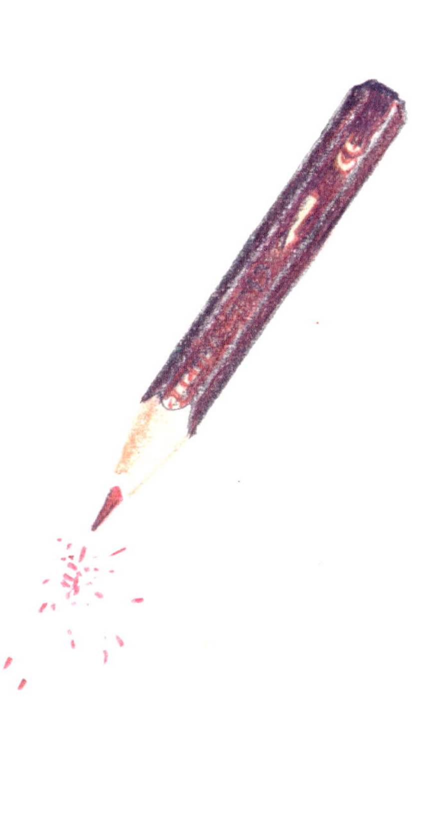

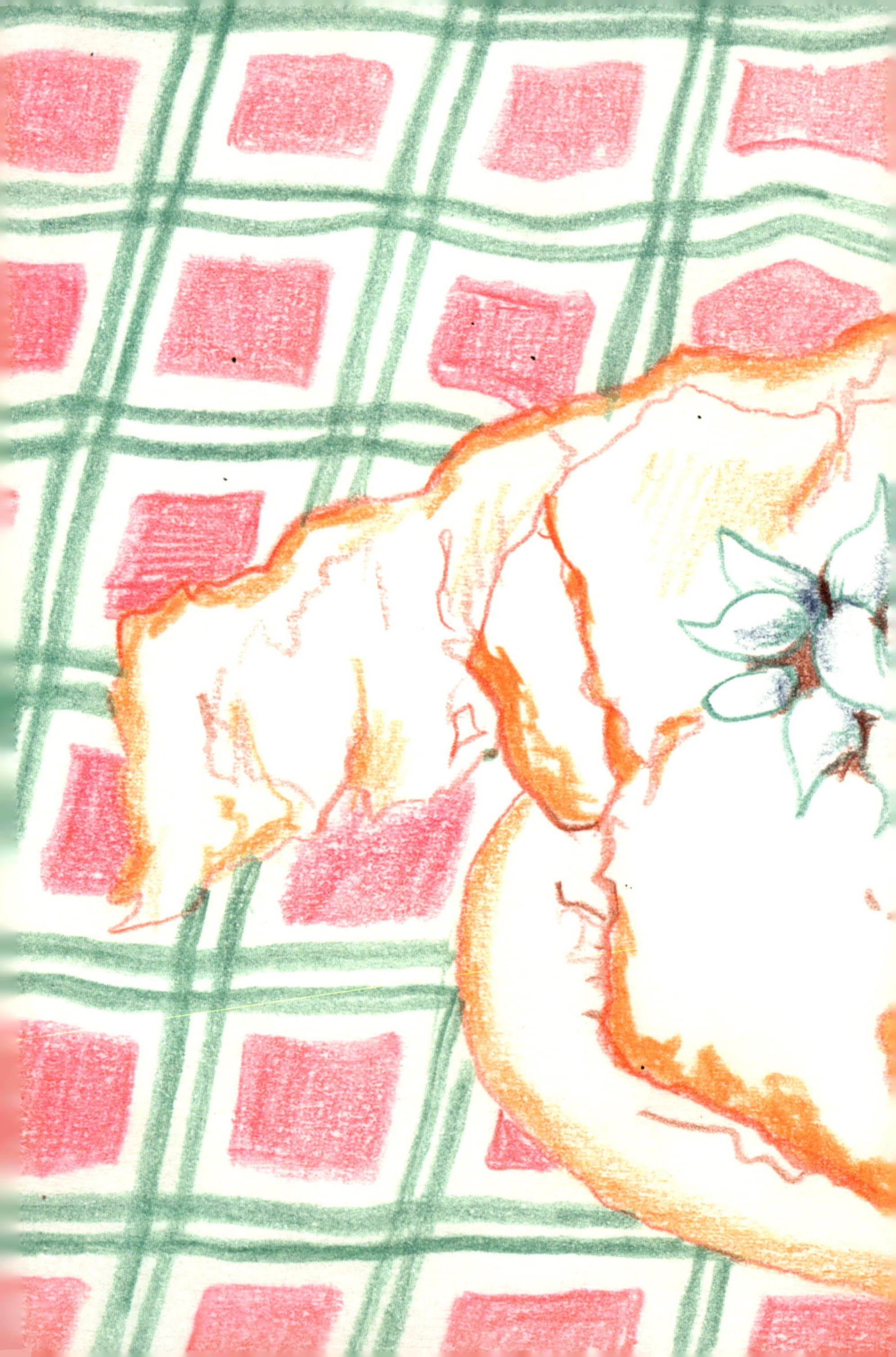

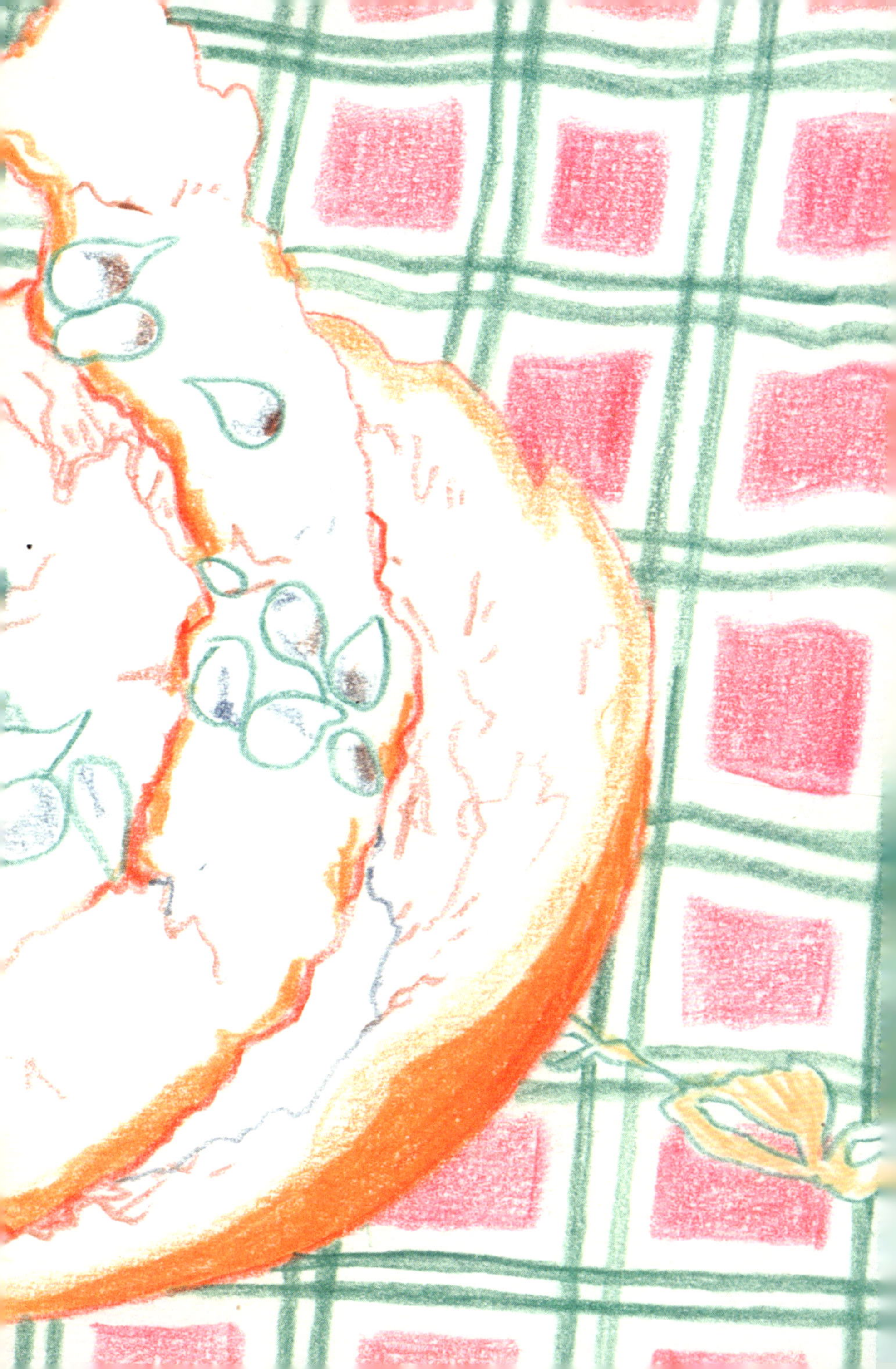

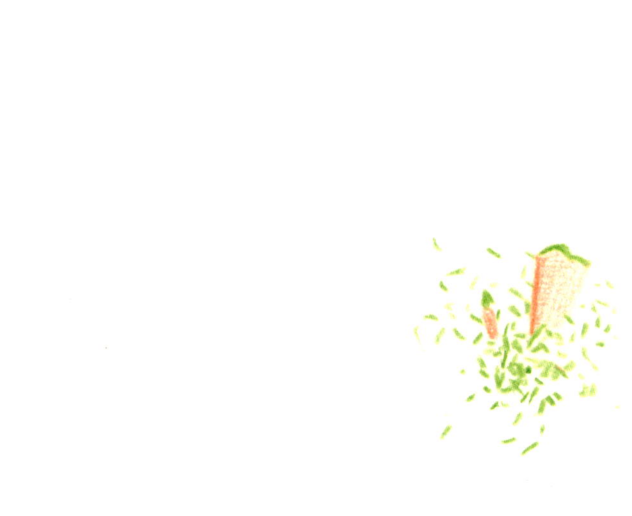

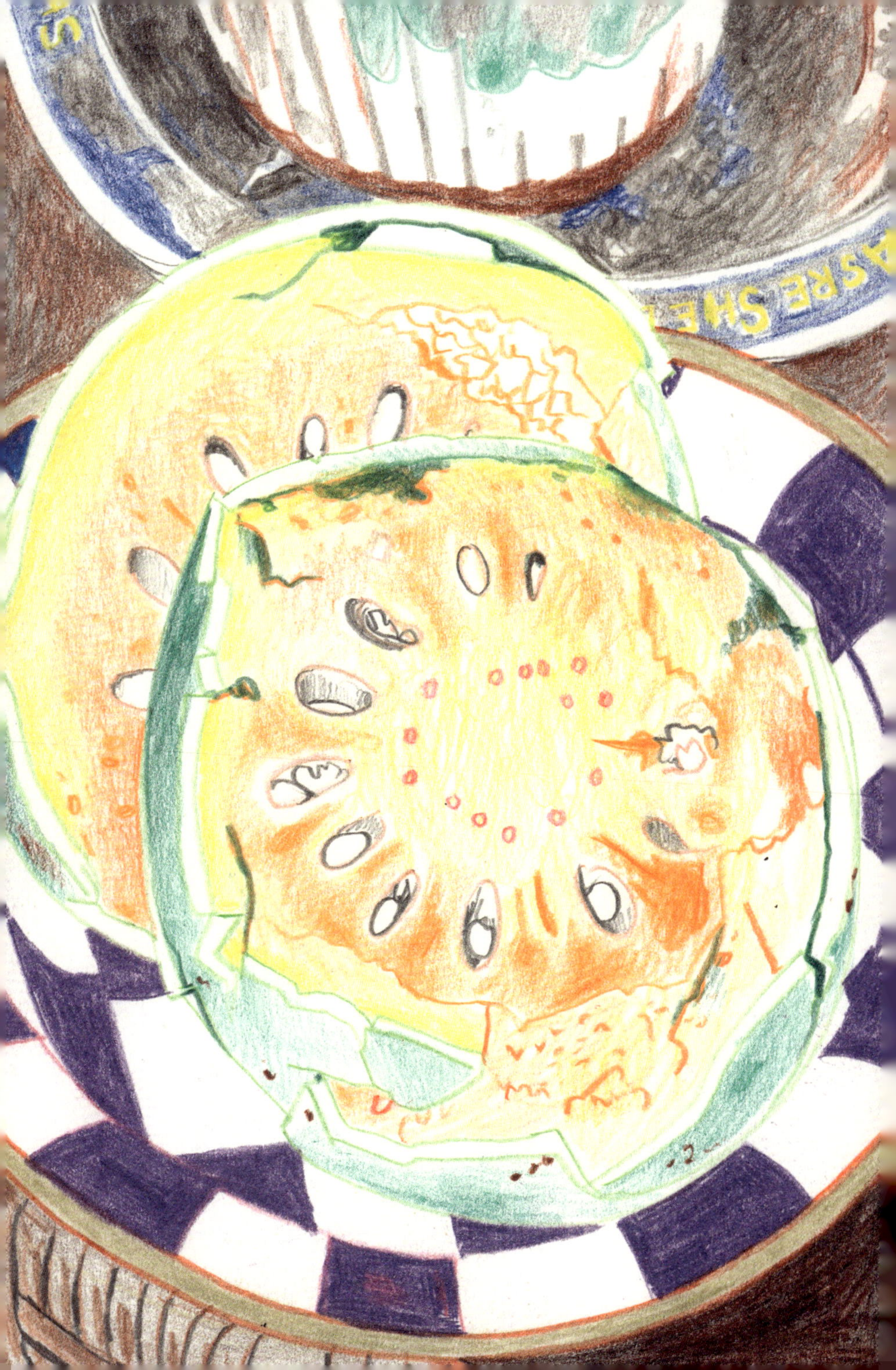

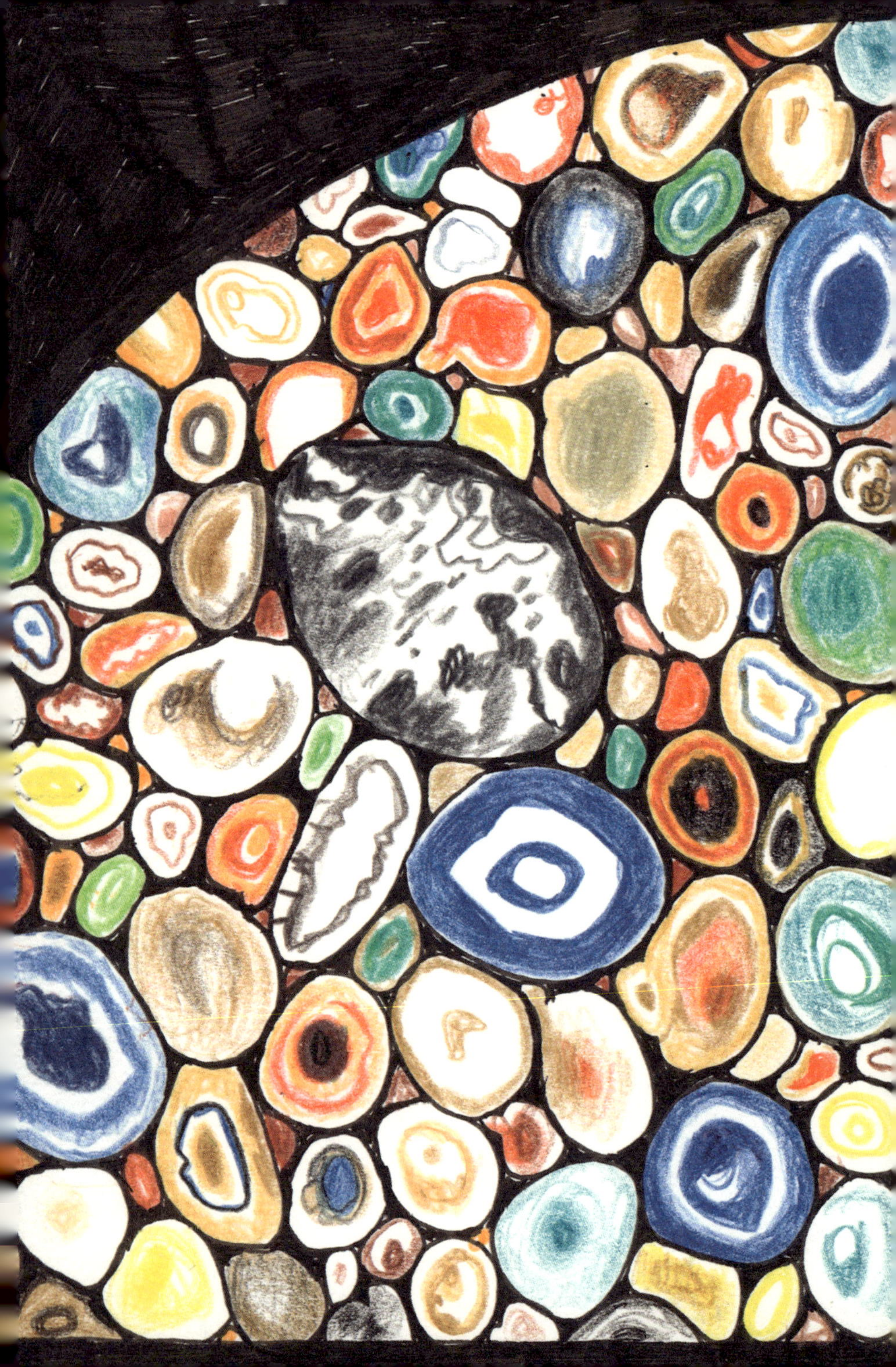

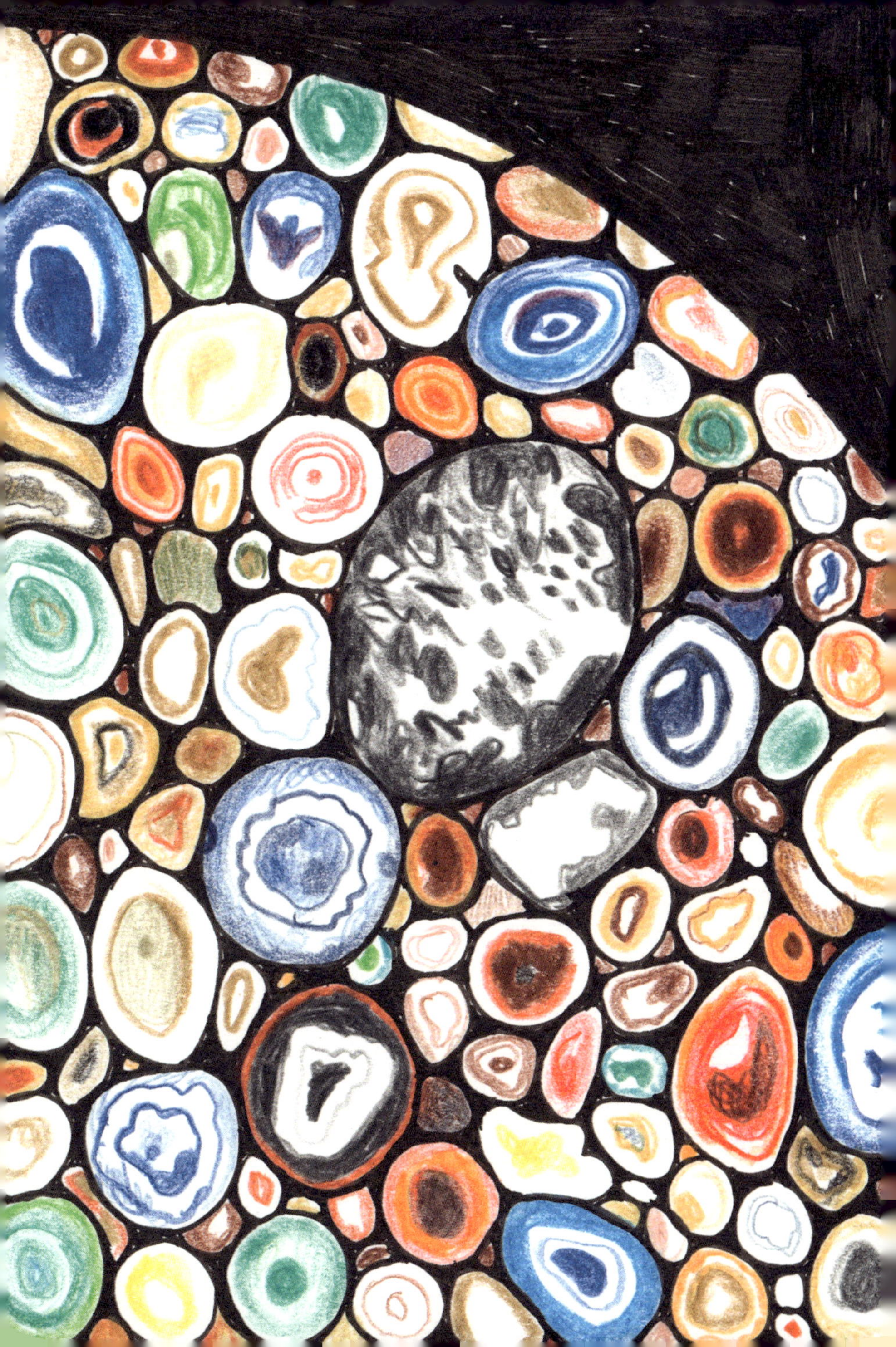

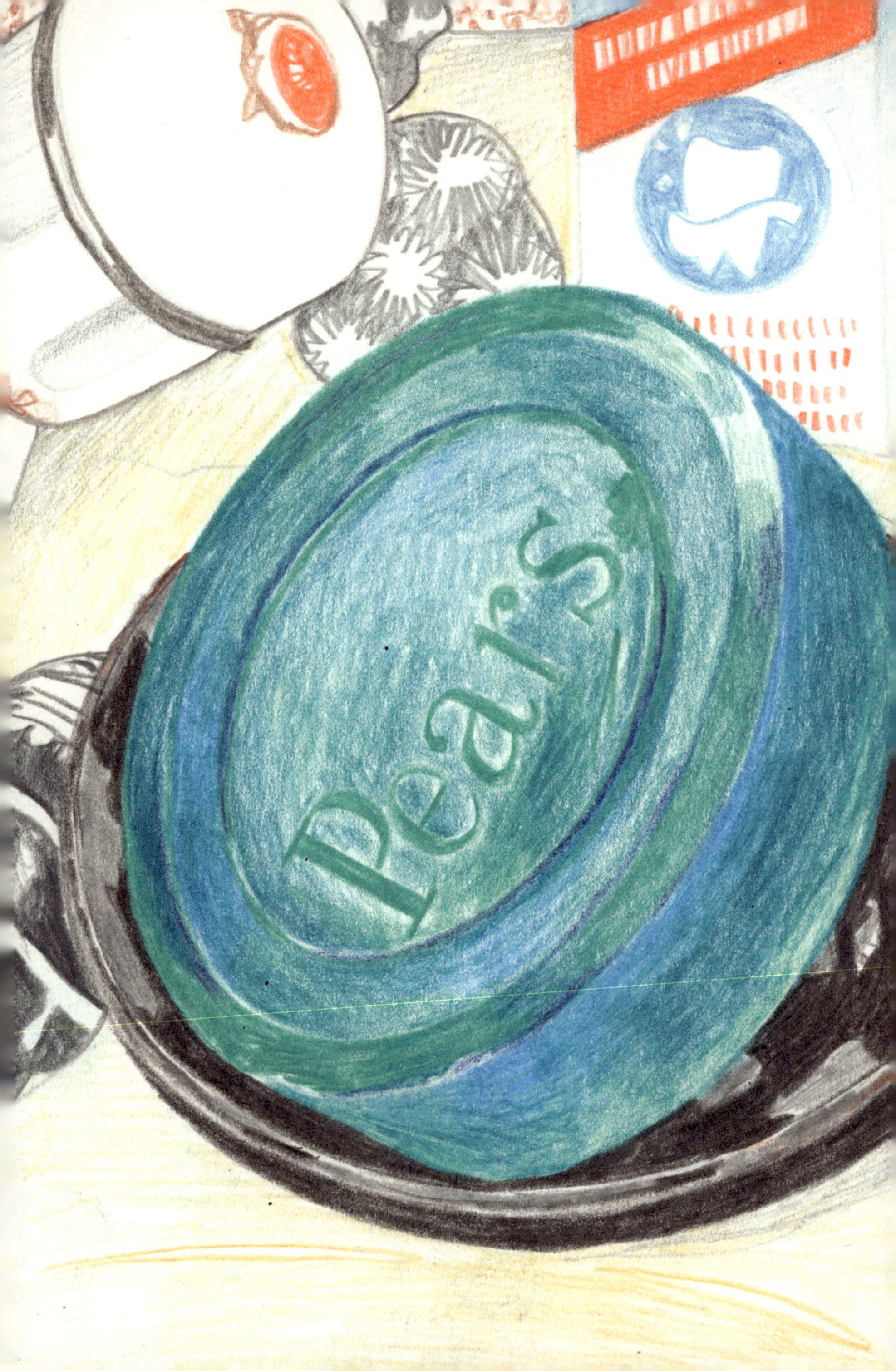
Pears

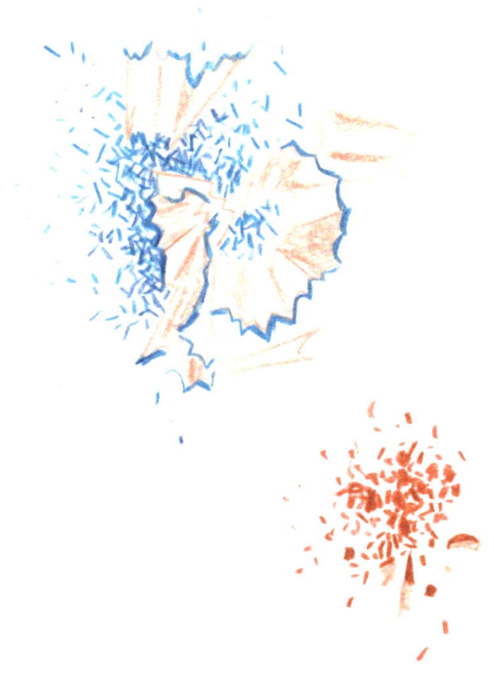

Crayons
Ingo Giezendanner

First Edition

On the Occasion of the Exhibition
Unkraut & Crayons by Ingo Giezendanner
at innen in Zurich, September 2022

Co-Published by Nieves and innen

www.nievesbooks.com
www.innenbooks.com
www.grrrr.net

ISBN 978-3-907179-53-6

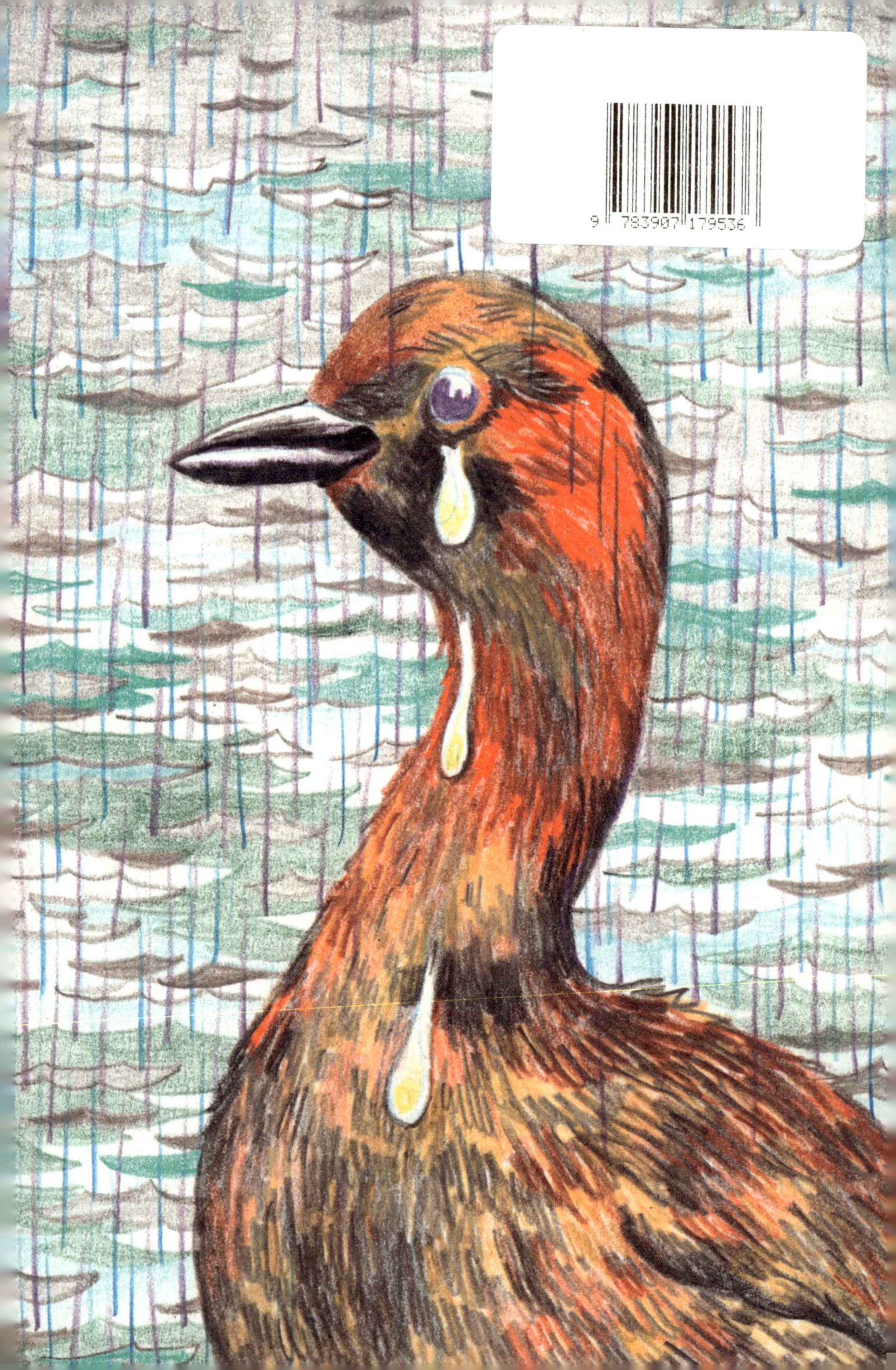
9 783907 179536